Sean O'Byrne

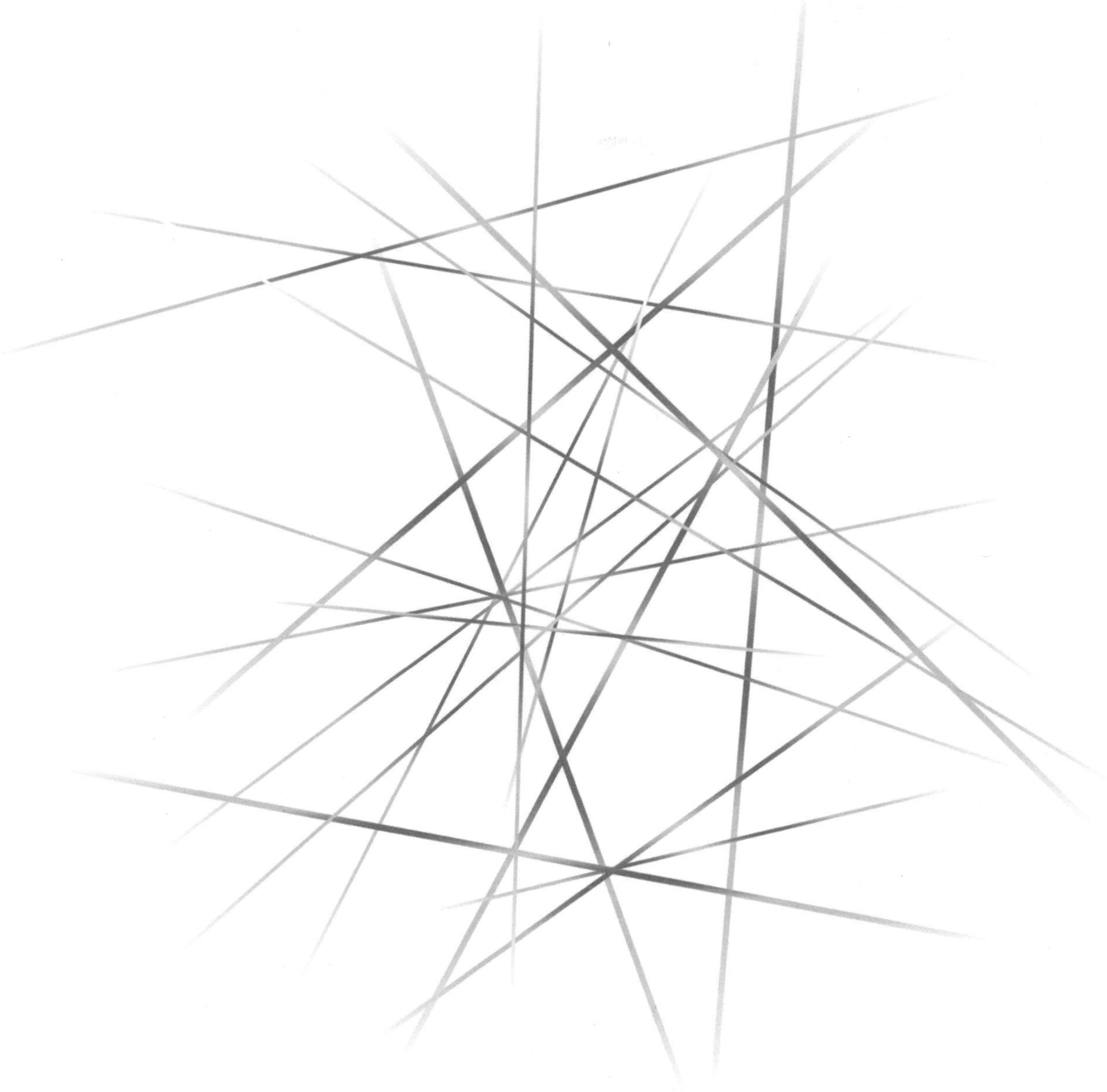

ESSENTIALS

GCSE ICT

Information & Communication Technology

Workbook

Contents

Hardware

Software and Development

Manipulating Data

Contents

Modern Living

Computer Systems

What is a Computer?

1. Which of the following statements about computers are true? Tick the correct options.

   A They need to be given instructions ☐ **B** They always have a keyboard ☐

   C They all process data ☐ **D** They all have a hard disk ☐

   E They all have a screen for output ☐ **F** They all have memory ☐

2. Which of the following statements about computer programs is true? Tick the correct option.

   A Programs contain instructions ☐

   B Programs are loaded by typing them in ☐

   C All programs can run on any computer ☐

   D All programs are stored on a computer's hard disk ☐

Personal Computers (PCs)

3. Which of these statements about netbooks are true? Tick the correct options.

   A They always have magnetic hard drives ☐ **B** They have webcams ☐

   C They have WiFi access ☐ **D** They have long battery life ☐

   E They usually have CD players ☐ **F** They're smaller than most laptops ☐

4. Which of the following items is commonly used to input into a PDA? Tick the correct option.

   A A mouse ☐ **B** A keyboard ☐

   C A touch pad ☐ **D** A joystick ☐

5. Give three suitable uses for a PDA.

   a) .... **b)** .... **c)** ....

6. Which of the following allow mobile phones to access the Internet? Tick the correct option.

   A MP3 ☐ **B** WAP ☐

   C PDF ☐ **D** HTM ☐

7. Which of the following is most likely to have a touch screen? Tick the correct option.

   A A laptop ☐ **B** A PDA ☐

   C A mainframe ☐ **D** A desktop PC ☐

Mainframe Computers

1. Circle the correct options in the following sentences.

   a) A supercomputer is most likely to be used for **predicting a weather forecast / working out a bank statement.**

   b) A collection of parts working together is called a **program / system**.

   c) A large multiuser computer is called a **PC / mainframe**.

   d) A series of instructions for a computer is called a **file / program**.

2. Fill in the missing words to complete the following sentences.

   The fastest computers of all are .... They're best at running programs very .... rather than running lots of programs at the ....

Computer Systems

3. Choose the correct words from the options given to complete the following sentences.

   webcam **personal** **netbook** **microphone** **computer**

   Desktop computers and laptops are both forms of ....

   A small laptop with Internet connectivity is called a .... This has visual input by means of a .... and sound input from a ....

4. Choose the correct words from the options given to complete the following sentences.

   embedded **microwave oven** **devices** **camera** **dedicated** **system**

   A computer that's designed to perform just one task is a .... computer. Computers like these are found in many electronic .... such as a .... and a .... Electronic control like this is called an ....

5. Circle the correct options in the following sentences.

   ASCII code is used by computers to store **numbers / characters**. An alternative system is more flexible and it's called **Monocode / Unicode**. Pictures are stored as a series of dots called **pixels / digits** and this type of storage is known as a **pixelated / bitmapped** file.

Hardware

Central Processing Unit (CPU)

1 According to Moore's Law, how often does the number of transistors in a processor double? Tick the correct option.

A One year ☐ **B** Two years ☐ **C** Three years ☐ **D** Four years ☐

2 Which part of the computer runs the programs? Tick the correct option.

A ROM ☐ **B** RAM ☐ **C** Control unit ☐ **D** ALU ☐

3 Circle the correct options in the following sentences.

a) All the main electronic components of a computer are plugged into the **motherboard / system card**.

b) All the contents of **RAM / ROM** are lost when the power is switched off.

c) A program compares the value of two items. This comparison takes place in the **control unit / arithmetic logic unit**.

d) A sound card is **software / hardware**.

4 Fill in the missing words to complete the following sentences.

The .... interprets and carries out program .... It's directed by the system ...., which determines how often an operation is carried out.

5 Fill in the correct words from the options given to complete the following sentences.

GHz **clock** **tick** **Hertz**

The processor contains a .... that controls the rate at which instructions are carried out. The speed is measured in multiples of .... This is 2.6 ...., which means that the timer will .... more than 2 billion times a second.

6 Match the following descriptions **1–5** to the correct answers **A–E**. Enter the appropriate numbers in the boxes provided.

1	Stores data on its way to the processor
2	1024 bytes
3	Where calculations are carried out
4	Where instructions are decoded and interpreted
5	A tiny switch in a processor

A Transistor ☐ **B** 1KB ☐

C Buffer ☐ **D** ALU ☐

E CU ☐

Memory

1. What part of RAM is used for queuing up data as it's being input? Tick the correct option.

   A A stack ☐ **B** A register ☐
   C A buffer ☐ **D** A sector ☐

2. What is the smallest unit of data in a computer system called? Tick the correct option.

   A One bit ☐ **B** One byte ☐
   C One nibble ☐ **D** One word ☐

3. A computer is advertised as having...

   > Memory: 3072MB 800MHz Dual Channel
   > DDR2 SDRAM (3x1024)

   Which of the following statements about the computer are true? Tick the correct options.

   A It has 3KB of RAM ☐ **B** It has 3MB of RAM ☐
   C It has over 3 billion bytes of memory ☐ **D** It has 3 billion bits of memory ☐
   E It has 3GB of memory ☐ **F** It has 3 billion kilobytes of memory ☐

4. Explain the connection between RAM and the processor when a program is running.

   ....

   ....

   ....

5. Choose the correct words from the options given to complete the following sentences.

   byte **ROM** **instructions** **booting** **RAM**

   One way to make a computer run faster is to give it more .... This will allow it to hold more .... in memory at the same time. Each location in memory usually holds one .... of data. When the computer starts, it first copies instructions from .... into main memory, a process called ....

Input Devices

Input Devices

1 Which of the following statements about input devices are true? Tick the correct options.

- **A** They convert physical energy into electrical signals
- **B** They produce digital signals
- **C** They send signals to output devices
- **D** They send signals to the computer's RAM
- **E** They are all concerned with getting data from humans into a computer

2 Which of the following is an input device? Tick the correct option.

- **A** A mouse
- **B** A printer
- **C** A memory stick
- **D** A motor

3 Which of the following is used for digitising an image? Tick the correct option.

- **A** A screen
- **B** A joystick
- **C** A touch pad
- **D** A scanner

Automated Data Input

4 Which of the following are reasons why data input is often automated? Tick the correct options.

- **A** It's quicker than manual input
- **B** It leads to fewer mistakes being made
- **C** It reduces the number of staff needed in data input centres
- **D** It allows many more ways of inputting data
- **E** It removes the need for input devices
- **F** It results in less paper being used

5 **a)** What do OMR and OCR stand for?

b) Explain the differences between OMR and OCR data input.

Automated Data Input (Cont.)

6 Look at the image below.

a) How is data stored on these cards so that it can be input into a computer?

b) Give two examples of where data is stored in this way.

7 Describe how RFID is used in supermarkets.

8 What is MICR used on? Tick the correct option.

A Gas bills ☐
B Exam papers ☐
C Cheques ☐
D Goods in supermarkets ☐

Sensors and Use of Sensors

9 Select the correct words from the options given to complete the following sentences.

digital **inductance** **analogue to digital converters** **touch sensitive** **analogue**

Sensors produce .... signals which have to be converted by .... to .... before they can be input into a computer. Traffic light systems often use .... in order to detect cars approaching a junction. Buttons in a lift are ....

10 Describe **two** common situations where sensors are used in everyday systems.

Output Devices

Output Devices

1 Which of the following is an example of output? Tick the correct option.

- **A** A mouse click
- **B** Hard copy
- **C** A scanned image
- **D** A signal from a sensor

Common Output Devices with PCs

2 Which of the following statements about output devices are true? Tick the correct options.

- **A** They convert physical energy into electrical signals
- **B** They always communicate with a human user
- **C** They take data from RAM
- **D** They make use of processed data
- **E** Computer systems are no use without them
- **F** They always send data to the processor

3 The following statements are about output devices. Tick whether each one is true or false.

Statement	True	False
a) Cathode ray tubes produce less heat than liquid crystal displays		
b) Cathode ray tubes take up less room on the desktop than TFT monitors		
c) Laser printers use toner powder		
d) Ink jet printers use expensive cartridges		
e) Dot matrix printers aren't used any more		
f) Dot matrix printers are quieter than ink jet printers		

4 Circle the correct options in the following sentences.

Garages often use **5-part / 3-part** stationery so that the customer can have a duplicate copy of an invoice. They use **dot matrix / square matrix** printers to print the invoices and the copies can be made because these are **laser / impact** printers. In supermarkets, **cold / thermal** printers use heat to make an image. **Laser / Radar** printers use powdered toner to make an image on the paper, which is then fixed to the paper using **pressure / heat**.

Common Output Devices with PCs (Cont.)

5 Match statements **1–10** to the correct output device **A–G**. Enter the appropriate number(s) in the boxes provided. Some examples may be used more than once.

1	Reduces the likelihood of feedback
2	Acts as an input as well as an output device
3	Uses pins to strike the paper
4	Uses heat to fix the image on paper
5	Produces a lot of heat when displaying an image
6	Useful with 3-part stationery
7	Used for the public to make train ticket enquiries
8	Produces warning noises when errors occur
9	Uses powdered toner
10	Uses liquid ink cartridges

A Dot matrix printer ☐ ☐

B Laser printer ☐ ☐

C Speakers ☐ ☐

D Headphones ☐ ☐

E Touch screen ☐ ☐

F CRT screen ☐ ☐

G Ink jet printer ☐ ☐

6 Henry is working from home. He uses online video communication and he also needs to produce high quality black and white hard copy. Describe the output devices that he needs and justify each one.

....

....

Specialist Output Devices

7 Which of the following produces paper output? Tick the correct option.

A A plotter ☐ **B** An actuator ☐

C A sensor ☐ **D** A light pen ☐

8 Which of the following might be output devices on a robot? Tick the correct options.

A A mechanical arm ☐ **B** A motor ☐ **C** An actuator ☐

D A light ☐ **E** A sensor ☐ **F** A speaker ☐

9 Describe **three** situations where motors are used to produce computer output.

....

....

....

Storage Devices

Memory

1 Which of the following is the binary equivalent of the number 2? Tick the correct option.

A 010 ☐ B 011 ☐

C 110 ☐ D 111 ☐

2 Which of the following is the smallest? Tick the correct option.

A 1 bit ☐ B 1 byte ☐

C 1 KB ☐ D 1 MB ☐

3 Which of these are ways to store characters? Tick the correct options.

A MP3 ☐ B JPEG ☐

C ASCII ☐ D Unicode ☐

E PDF ☐ F HTML ☐

4 The following statements are about storage. Tick whether each one is true or false.

Statement	True	False
a) Pictures are converted to pixels before storage		
b) Bitmaps are a way to store sounds		
c) Computer programs are stored as a series of bytes		
d) 1 megabyte is 1024 bytes		
e) 1 gigabyte is 1024 megabytes		
f) 1 character takes 1 KB of storage		

5 Select the correct words from the options given to complete the following sentences.

samples 1 byte numbers 8

A bit can be either 0 or .... Bits are grouped together in most computers. .... bits usually represent 1 .... Music can be stored digitally by taking .... at regular intervals and storing .... to represent loudness and pitch.

Memory (Cont.)

6 Circle the correct options in the following sentences.

a) 01000001 is the binary equivalent of **64 / 65**.

b) Each column in a binary number is worth **2 / 10** times as much as its neighbour on the right.

c) Music can be stored in **MP3 / JPEG** format.

d) One way that a computer knows what stored data means is by its **location / size**.

e) Unicode is a way of storing **pictures / letters**.

Primary Storage

7 The following statements are about RAM. Tick whether each one is true or false.

Statement	True	False
a) RAM stores program instructions after the computer is switched off		
b) Program instructions are copied to RAM before they can be carried out		
c) RAM stores data that's being worked on		
d) RAM holds data that's on its way to the processor		
e) There's usually less RAM than ROM in a PC		
f) RAM can't be written to by the processor		

8 Which of the following are functions of ROM? Tick the correct options.

A Stores boot-up instructions ☐

B Stores currently running programs in a PC ☐

C Stores data being worked on ☐

D Stores input / output instructions ☐

E Used to store programs in electronic devices ☐

F Can be written to ☐

9 Explain why flash memory is often used instead of hard drives in some PCs.

....

....

Secondary Storage

Secondary Storage

1. Which of the following are examples of secondary storage? Tick the correct options.

   A Storing data for the future ☐
   B Storing data that's being worked on ☐
   C Holding instructions as they're being processed ☐
   D Taking back ups ☐
   E Storing data that isn't wanted again ☐
   F Increasing the size of programs that can be run ☐

2. Which of the following are advantages of using USB memory sticks? Tick the correct options.

   A They're small ☐
   B They only hold a small amount of data ☐
   C They're robust ☐
   D They can be re-written ☐
   E They hold more data than hard disks ☐
   F They use magnetic technology ☐

3. Which of these are examples of flash memory? Tick the correct options.

   A Hard disks ☐
   B CD-ROM ☐
   C A camera memory card ☐
   D A telephone SIM card ☐
   E A USB memory stick ☐
   F A DVD ☐

4. Match the following descriptions **1–5** to the storage methods **A–D**. Enter the appropriate number(s) in the boxes provided.

1	An optical method
2	The largest magnetic store in most PCs
3	Used for backup but is slow
4	Uses shorter wavelength light than CD
5	The use of a hard disk as an extension to RAM

   A Blu Ray ☐ ☐
   B Hard disk ☐ ☐
   C Tape ☐ ☐
   D Virtual memory ☐ ☐

Virtual Memory

1 Explain why virtual memory is needed in a PC.

....

....

2 Circle the correct options in the following sentences.

a) Virtual memory makes use of **RAM / a disk** to store parts of a program that aren't currently needed.

b) When it's needed, a part of a program is loaded into **ROM / RAM**.

c) A program that uses virtual memory runs **faster / slower** than a program that's entirely resident in RAM.

Optical and Magnetic Storage

3 Which of the following are examples of optical storage? Tick the correct options.

A Hard disks	☐	**B** CD-ROM	☐
C A camera memory card	☐	**D** Blu Ray	☐
E A USB memory stick	☐	**F** A DVD	☐

4 Which of the following are examples of magnetic storage? Tick the correct options.

A Hard disks	☐	**B** CD-ROM	☐
C A camera memory card	☐	**D** A tape	☐
E A USB memory stick	☐	**F** A DVD	☐

Online Storage

5 Which of the following are advantages of a company using Software as a Service? Tick the correct options.

A It's cheaper than owning your own software ☐

B It makes upgrades easier to manage ☐

C It reduces the need for a lot of servers ☐

D It avoids the need to buy licenses ☐

E It avoids the need to pay for software ☐

F It reduces the amount of software used by the company ☐

Portable Computing

Range of Portable Devices

1. Which of the following are methods of connecting a mobile phone with a PC? Tick the correct options.

   A WAP ☐ **B** Bluetooth ☐ **C** WiMAX ☐

   D WiFi ☐ **E** LAN ☐ **F** Cable ☐

2. The following statements are about mobile phones. Tick whether each one is true or false.

Statement	True	False
a) They contain RAM		
b) They can work anywhere		
c) They need to be within range of a base station to work		
d) They can be used to access email		
e) They can play MP3 files		
f) They allow totally secure communication		

3. What is a small computer with WiFi, webcam, speakers and microphones called? Tick the correct option.

   A A desktop ☐ **B** A PDA ☐

   C A smartphone ☐ **D** A netbook ☐

4. Circle the correct options in the following sentences.

   Lightweight computers often have the same features as bigger **iPod / desktop** machines. They can connect with lots of devices via their **USB / hard drive** ports and their **card / memory** readers let them access images from a digital camera. They can use **HiFi / WiFi** to connect to local area networks without the need for cables, and **Redtooth / Bluetooth** allows them to communicate with other enabled devices that are located nearby.

5. The following statements are about small computer systems. Tick whether each one is true or false.

Statement	True	False
a) Using proprietary operating systems, such as Windows™, keeps costs down		
b) They can save weight by using hard drives		
c) CD drives add considerably to the weight of small computers		
d) Battery life is rarely a problem		
e) Solid state memory can be used instead of a hard disk		
f) An external keyboard can make typing easier		

Range of Portable Devices (Cont.)

6 Match descriptions **1–5** to the options given **A–E**. Enter the appropriate numbers in the boxes provided.

1	A dot that makes up a picture
2	A measure of the clarity of an image
3	A video file format
4	A sound file format
5	Storage used in a camera

A Flash memory ☐ **B** MP3 ☐
C Pixel ☐ **D** Resolution ☐
E WMV ☐

7 Select the correct words from the options given to complete the following sentences.

download **compressed** **pixels** **files** **storage**

A high quality image requires more .... than a low quality one. It's made up of more .... and so it's often .... in order to reduce the size of the .... This can reduce the final quality of the image, but it will decrease .... times.

8 What is the minimum number of satellites needed to locate a sat nav system on the Earth's surface? Tick the correct option.

A 1 ☐ **B** 2 ☐ **C** 3 ☐ **D** 4 ☐

9 What does GPS stands for? Tick the correct option.

A Global Pointing System ☐ **B** Global Personal Service ☐
C Global Positioning System ☐ **D** Global Personal Security ☐

10 Explain how a GPS system can be used to produce a display on a car's sat nav screen.

....

....

....

Portable Computing

Connectivity Technologies

1 What is a protocol? Tick the correct option.

A A way to program computers ☐
B A set of rules ☐
C A communication device ☐
D A type of network ☐

2 Why do we need protocols in computer networks?

....

....

3 Which of the following are wireless methods of communication? Tick the correct options.

A LAN ☐
B Bluetooth ☐
C A parallel port ☐
D WiFi ☐
E A network cable ☐
F A switch ☐

4 What is the maximum distance over which Bluetooth can communicate? Tick the correct option.

A 1 metre ☐
B 10 metres ☐
C 100 metres ☐
D 1000 metres ☐

5 What is a connection point for a WiFi enabled network? Tick the correct option.

A A hotspot ☐
B A hub ☐
C An interface ☐
D A LAN ☐

6 Explain why delegates are provided with WiFi at meetings.

....

....

....

7 Some cities aim to provide WiFi access throughout the city area. Explain why they would want to do this.

....

....

....

Connectivity Technologies (Cont.)

8 Which of the following are possible with a WiFi enabled network? Tick the correct options.

- **A** Controlling household gadgets
- **B** Allowing access to anyone up to a mile away
- **C** Allowing only selected computers to access it
- **D** Allowing an unlimited number of computers effective access
- **E** Restricting logins to authorised people
- **F** Allowing open access to any user

9 The following statements are about WiFi. Tick whether each one is true or false.

Statement	True	False
a) It makes no difference if buildings are in the way between the user and the network		
b) It's just as fast as a wired network		
c) It's just as secure as a wired network		
d) It requires no installation or building work		
e) The distance between a user and the network makes no difference		
f) It can be accessed via a router		

Mobile Broadband

10 Which of the following statements about mobile broadband are true? Tick the correct options.

- **A** It's free
- **B** It's just as fast as a wired network
- **C** It works anywhere
- **D** It doesn't require payment to a hotspot provider
- **E** It requires signing up to a communications provider
- **F** It works through mobile phone base stations

Portable Computing

Bandwidth

1 What is bandwidth? Tick the correct option.

- **A** The range of frequencies in a communication link ☐
- **B** The amount of data received by a device ☐
- **C** The size of a computer's memory ☐
- **D** The speed of transmission of data ☐

2 Which of the following is the same as 1000 bits per second? Tick the correct option.

A 1 mbps ☐ **B** 1 kbps ☐ **C** 1 gbps ☐ **D** 1 tbps ☐

3 Which of the following connection rates could be regarded as broadband? Tick the correct options.

A 1 kbps ☐ **B** 100 kbps ☐ **C** 256 kbps ☐

D 1 mbps ☐ **E** 1000 bps ☐ **F** 2 mbps ☐

4 Explain why broadband is needed when transferring music files across the Internet.

....

....

Protocols

5 Which of the following are related to the sending of emails? Tick the correct options.

A VoIP ☐ **B** POP ☐ **C** IMAP ☐

D PDF ☐ **E** HTTP ☐ **F** FTP ☐

6 The following statements are about communications protocols. Tick whether each one is true or false.

Statement	True	False
a) VoIP is concerned with making telephone calls over the Internet		
b) TCP/IP is only concerned with the sending of web pages		
c) HTTPS is a secure way of sending data in web pages		
d) Web pages sent by HTTP are encrypted		
e) POP works together with TCP/IP		
f) SMTP is concerned with sending images in web pages		

Protocols (Cont.)

7 Circle the correct options in the following sentences.

a) Encryption is the process of changing data so that it's **smaller / unreadable**.

b) Encryption is used when sending **orders / credit card details** over the Internet.

c) Decryption requires the recipient to have a **code / key**.

d) A secure web page has a **padlock / letter 's'** at the bottom.

Problems with Portable Computing

8 Which of these methods can be used to secure a home wireless router? Tick the correct options.

A Use WEP ▢

B Keep the router in a cupboard ▢

C Don't broadcast the SSID ▢

D Don't restrict the MAC addresses allowed ▢

E Use WPA2 ▢

F Don't encrypt the signals ▢

9 Select the correct words from the list to complete the following sentences.

encrypt **hacker** **key** **wired**

Wireless data transmissions are easier for a .... to intercept than in a .... network because the transmissions can pass through walls. It's a good idea to .... the transmissions so that the data can't be understood without having a ....

10 Explain why the performance of a person's computer may be slowed down when there are many users connected to a single WiFi hot spot.

....

....

....

....

Networks

Why Network?

1. What is each device connected to a network called? Tick the correct option.

   A A computer ☐ **B** A client ☐
   C A network card ☐ **D** A node ☐

2. Which of the following are benefits of networking computers? Tick the correct options.

   A Peripherals can be shared ☐
   B Data can be shared ☐
   C Software costs less ☐
   D Communication is easier across a network ☐
   E The computers run faster ☐
   F Networked computers cost less than stand-alone computers ☐

3. What is distributed processing?

   ....

4. Explain why a network can reduce the amount of effort spent on upgrading software.

   ....

   ....

5. What is the purpose of having a login ID? Tick the correct options.

   A It allows the network operating system to record your activity ☐
   B It determines what network resources are available to you ☐
   C It takes the place of a password ☐
   D It connects you to the right server ☐
   E It stops others from accessing your files ☐
   F It protects your files from malware ☐

6. Explain why running a network can be expensive for a company.

   ....

Components

1 The following statements are about network components. Tick whether each one is true or false.

Statement	True	False
a) Every device connected to a network needs a network interface card		
b) Fibre optic cable is more resistant to weather than metal cable		
c) Fibre optic cable can only transmit one data channel		
d) Wireless components require no building work to install		
e) Wireless networks are more secure than wired networks		
f) Wireless networks transmit data faster than cable networks		

2 Select the correct words from the options given to complete the following sentences.

encrypt **hub** **VPN** **infrastructure** **switch**

A .... is a passive device that connects many nodes to a network. A .... is able to direct data to specific parts of a network. A .... allows a company to have the services of a network without having to own the .... For security, it then has to .... its data when using the network.

3 Explain why more companies are using external companies to provide network services.

....

....

....

4 Select the correct words from the options given to complete the following sentences.

collisions **length** **bus** **all** **part** **star**

A .... network is cheap to set up but it can only be a limited .... It often performs slowly because it's subject to many .... If a cable is disconnected, ... of the network is affected. A .... network is set up differently, so if a cable is disconnected only .... of the network is affected.

Types of Network

LAN and WAN

1 Which of these statements about a LAN are true? Tick the correct options.

- **A** A LAN is confined to one site ☐
- **B** A LAN is totally under the control of its owners ☐
- **C** A LAN makes use of national telephone lines ☐
- **D** A LAN can be part of the Internet ☐
- **E** A LAN can cover the world ☐
- **F** A LAN has to be connected with cables ☐

2 Select the correct words from the options given to complete the following sentences.

leased **network** **line** **public** **large** **telecoms**

A WAN is a .... that extends over a .... geographical area. It makes use of .... communication links such as those provided by .... companies. Sometimes a .... is rented exclusively by a company to provide access to the links.

Different Networks and Topology

3 Match the descriptions of types of network **1–5** to the correct answers **A–E**. Enter the appropriate number in the boxes provided.

1	A network where all the computers have equal status
2	A computer that requests services from a server on a network
3	A powerful computer that provides file storage facilities on a network
4	A device that links computers together on a network
5	The way in which computers are laid out in a network

- **A** Topology ☐
- **B** Peer-to-peer ☐
- **C** Server ☐
- **D** Client ☐
- **E** Hub ☐

4 Explain how a peer-to-peer network can be used to share music files illegally on the Internet.

....

....

Different Networks and Topology (Cont.)

5 The diagram shows the layout of a network.

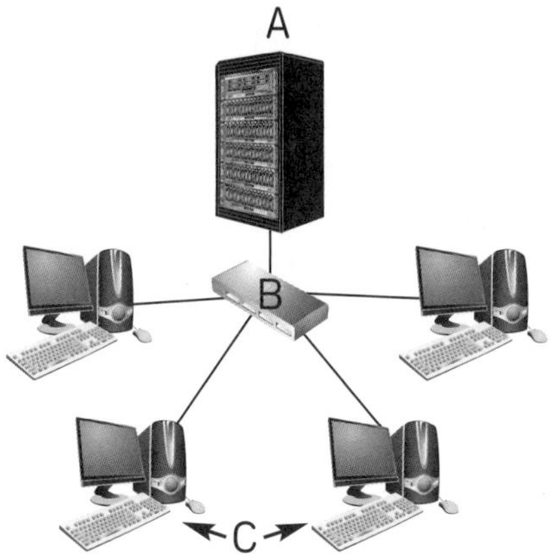

a) Identify the components A, B and C.

A: ....

B: ....

C: ....

b) What network topology is shown here? ....

6 The diagram shows the layout of another network.

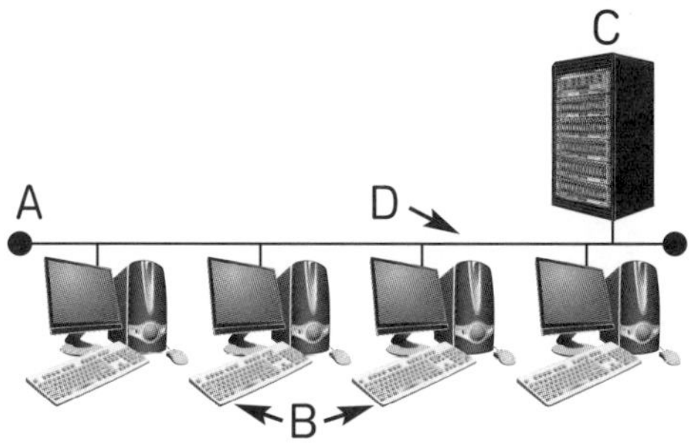

a) Identify the components A, B, C and D.

A: ....

B: ....

C: ....

D: ....

b) What network topology is shown here? ....

7 State three advantages of setting up a network in a star formation.

....

....

8 Explain why ring networks are uncommon.

....

....

Software

Software

1. What is software? Tick the correct option.

- **A** Computer programs ☐
- **B** Instruction manuals ☐
- **C** Data ☐
- **D** The settings on a computer ☐

2. Select the correct words from the options given to complete the following sentences.

backing storage **RAM** **instructions** **processor** **hard disk** **run**

A computer program is a set of .... These are normally stored on .... such as the .... They are copied into .... when the program is .... and they're then carried out by the ....

3. Where are program instructions decoded? Tick the correct option.

- **A** RAM ☐
- **B** ROM ☐
- **C** The processor ☐
- **D** The hard disk ☐

System Software and Utilities

4. Which of the following can be regarded as system software? Tick the correct options.

- **A** An editor ☐
- **B** A spreadsheet ☐
- **C** A compiler ☐
- **D** A controller for a microwave cooker ☐
- **E** The program controlling traffic lights ☐
- **F** A text editor ☐

5. Which of the following are utilities? Tick the correct options.

- **A** An editor ☐
- **B** A defragmenter ☐
- **C** A word processor ☐
- **D** A database system ☐
- **E** Compression software ☐
- **F** A PDF reader ☐

Applications

1 Which of the following are applications? Tick the correct options.

- **A** A spreadsheet ☐
- **B** A loader ☐
- **C** A compiler ☐
- **D** A payroll processing package ☐
- **E** A program that controls a washing machine ☐
- **F** A printer driver ☐

2 Select the correct words from the options given to complete the following sentences.

spreadsheets **word processing packages** **application** **DBMSs** **generic**

An .... is a program that does a useful job for us. Some are so useful that there are lots of similar competing products on the market. These are called .... software. For example, there are .... for creating and editing documents, ... for manipulating rows and columns of figures, and .... for creating and managing large volumes of data.

Specialised Software (Open Source and Proprietary)

3 The following statements are about software. Tick whether each one is true or false.

Statement	True	False
a) Specially written software takes longer to get than off-the-shelf software		
b) Specially written software is cheaper than off-the-shelf software		
c) Specially written software is more reliable than off-the-shelf software		
d) Specially written software is easier to use than off-the-shelf software		
e) Specially written software is used by more users than off-the-shelf software		
f) Specially written software often has more bugs than off-the-shelf software		

Operating Systems

Operating Systems and Device Drivers

1 Which of the following are purposes of an operating system? Tick the correct options.

- **A** It provides a way for the user to control the computer ☐
- **B** It removes the need to have different applications ☐
- **C** It saves space on the hard disk ☐
- **D** It makes sure that your files can be read by any computer ☐
- **E** It removes the need to understand the internal workings of the computer ☐
- **F** It makes it easier for programmers to write applications ☐

2 The diagram shows how a user can interact with the computer hardware when carrying out a task. The diagram shows how everything is connected. Use the words below to identify boxes **a)–c)**.

Application **Operating system** **User**

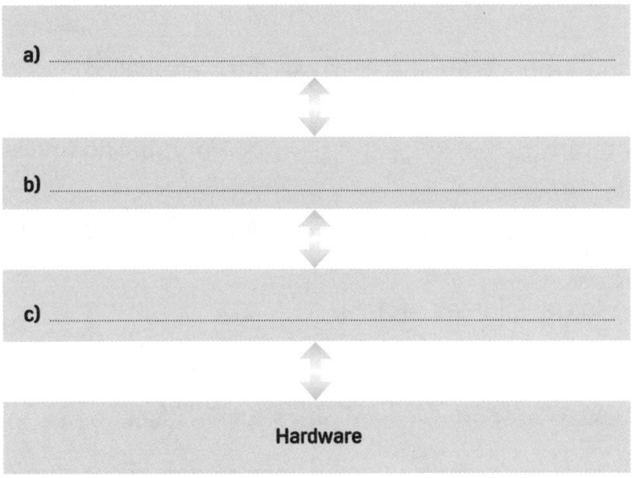

3 The following statements are about operating systems. Tick whether each one is true or false.

Statement	True	False
a) They manage the memory of a computer		
b) They control the sending of data to a printer		
c) They control the shutter speed of a digital camera		
d) They carry out program instructions		
e) They load programs into memory		
f) They provide a way of deleting files		

Types of Operating System

1 Match the descriptions of types of operating system **1–5** to the correct answers **A–E**. Enter the appropriate number in the boxes provided.

1	Requires the collection together of all the jobs, then it does them one after another
2	Allows a 'conversation' to be had with the computer
3	Allows an immediate response to inputs
4	Allows more than one program to be in RAM at a time
5	Allows computers to work together

A Network ☐
B Batch ☐
C Interactive ☐
D Multiprogramming ☐
E Real time ☐

2 Which of the following require a real-time operating system? Tick the correct options.

A Processing of exam results ☐
B A computer game ☐
C An autopilot ☐
D A traffic light controller ☐
E A payroll system ☐
F A stock control system ☐

3 Select the correct words from the options given to complete the following sentences.

run **RAM** **programs** **processor** **multiprogramming**

Most computers allow many programs to be resident in .... at the same time.

They can appear to .... at the same time. This is called ....,

but in fact the .... just switches its attention between the different

.... very quickly.

4 Which of the following require a batch processing operating system? Tick the correct options.

A Processing of exam results ☐
B A computer game ☐
C An autopilot ☐
D A traffic light controller ☐
E A payroll system ☐
F A stock control system ☐

Operating Systems

Examples of Operating Systems

1 Which of the following is an Open Source operating system? Tick the correct option.

A Windows™ ☐ **B** Linux ☐ **C** Unix ☐ **D** Firefox ☐

2 Which of the following are possible reasons to upgrade an operating system? Tick the correct options.

- **A** The new version might be easier to use ☐
- **B** The new version might have more features ☐
- **C** The new version might need new applications ☐
- **D** The new version might have a more complex interface ☐
- **E** The new version might be backwards incompatible ☐
- **F** The new version might not use icons ☐

3 Why do operating systems often automatically download updates? Tick the correct options.

- **A** To fix bugs ☐
- **B** To improve security ☐
- **C** To save distribution costs ☐
- **D** To add new features ☐
- **E** To reduce the size of the software ☐
- **F** To improve compatibility with other operating systems ☐

4 Which of the following statements correctly describes Open Source software? Tick the correct options.

- **A** You have to compile it yourself ☐
- **B** You can get hold of the source code ☐
- **C** It's more expensive than proprietary software ☐
- **D** It's often updated by enthusiasts ☐
- **E** It runs on any computer ☐
- **F** It isn't available for Windows™ computers ☐

Files

5 Suggest **three** pieces of advice that you would give about choosing a name for a file you are saving.

....

....

....

Files (Cont.)

6 A web resource has the following URL: http://www.microsoft.com/en/us/default.aspx

a) What is the name of the file being accessed? ....

b) What is the path of this resource? ....

7 The diagram shows how a hard disk is organised.

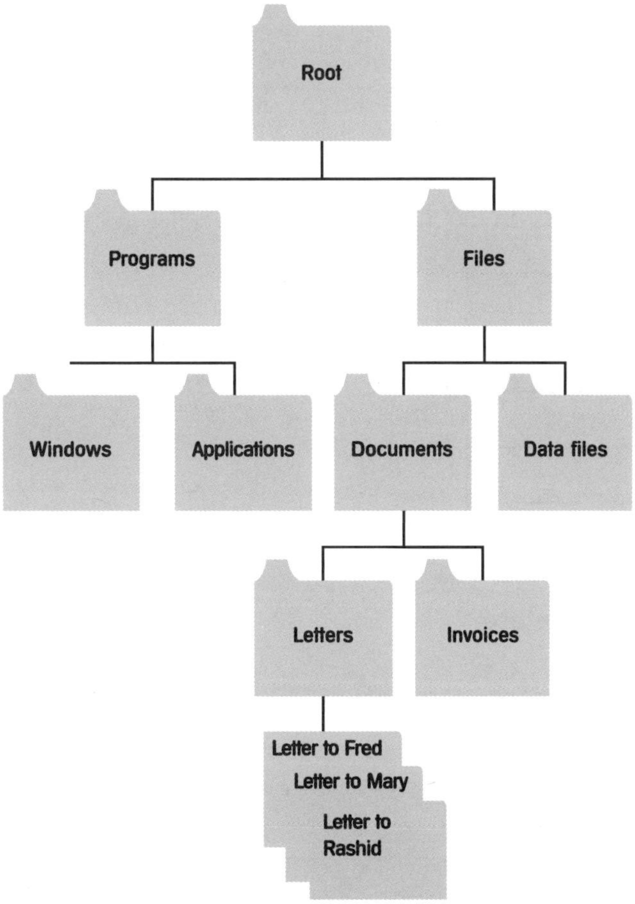

a) How many folders are shown? ....

b) How many files are shown? ....

8 **a)** Describe what is meant by a **folder hierarchy**.

....

....

b) Describe **two** advantages of using a folder hierarchy.

....

....

User Interfaces

Interfaces

1 This is a screen shot of an interface.

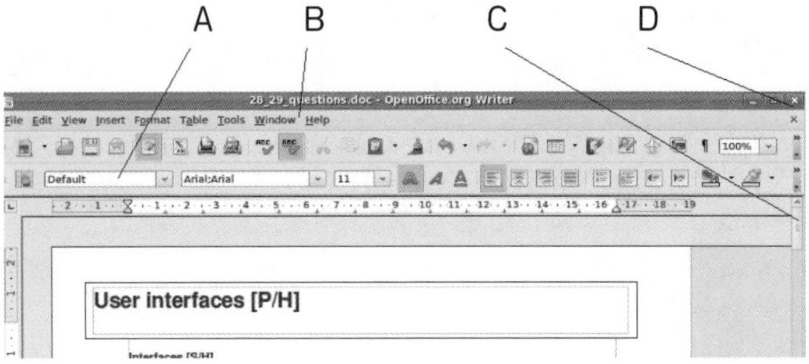

a) What type of interface is this? Tick the correct option.

A Command line ☐

B Menu driven ☐

C Touch ☐

D GUI ☐

b) Identify the following items on the interface. Write the letter in the box that corresponds to each item.

Interface Items	Letter
Close button	
Menu bar	
Scroll bar	
Drop-down box	

2 What is meant by a **user interface**?

....

....

GUIs and their Features

3 Select the correct words from the options given to complete the following sentences.

graphical **files** **icons** **intuitive** **mouse**

Users interact with most PCs via pictures known as .... These can represent programs or .... and you select them by using the .... This is called a .... interface and is usually an easy or .... way to control a computer.

GUIs and their Features (Cont.)

4 Match the following descriptions of screen controls **1–5** to the correct answers **A–E**. Enter the appropriate numbers in the boxes provided.

1	It allows several settings to be accepted in one action
2	It allows choices to be made from limited options by selecting words
3	It causes the computer to carry out a chosen action when clicked
4	It allows only one of a set of choices to be selected
5	It presents a set of choices that lead to further choices

A Drop-down menu ☐

B Command button ☐

C Drop-down list box ☐

D Radio button ☐

E Dialogue box ☐

5 Explain how screen controls make it easier to learn how to use a new piece of software.

....

....

6 What is the difference between a menu and a toolbar? ....

....

Hyperlinks, Hotspots and Other Interfaces

7 Circle the correct options in the following sentences.

a) An interface where the user has to type instructions is called a **command line / graphical** interface.

b) A part of a web page which, when clicked, takes you to another location is called a **hyperlink / text box**.

c) Command line interfaces react more **quickly / slowly** than graphical interfaces.

d) Cash machines make use of **command line / menu** interfaces.

8 Explain why computer professionals often prefer to work with command line interfaces.

....

....

Teams and System Life Cycle

IT Jobs, People and Teams

1. Who of the following is responsible for delivering a new IT system on time and within budget? Tick the correct option.

   A The analyst ☐ **B** The project manager ☐
   C The operations manager ☐ **D** The programmer ☐

2. Which of the following jobs are likely to be carried out by IT technicians? Tick the correct options.

   A Installing software ☐
   B Deciding which software to buy ☐
   C Writing program code ☐
   D Carrying out repairs ☐
   E Devising a software solution to a problem ☐
   F Maintaining equipment in good order ☐

3. Describe the role of the help desk in an organisation.

   ....

   ....

4. Which of the following jobs are likely to be carried out by an analyst? Tick the correct options.

   A Installing software ☐ **B** Investigating a problem ☐
   C Writing program code ☐ **D** Assessing the feasibility of a project ☐
   E Defining a solution to a problem ☐ **F** Testing the finished solution ☐

The System Life Cycle

5. Which of the following are common reasons why IT projects sometimes go wrong? Tick the correct options.

   A The customer may have unrealistic expectations ☐
   B The developer finds it hard to communicate with the programmers ☐
   C The developer doesn't communicate well with the customer ☐
   D Too many programming languages are used ☐
   E There's insufficient consultation between the developers and the customer ☐
   F The solution is developed on a different platform from the customer's ☐

The System Life Cycle (Cont.)

6 The diagram shows some of the stages of the system life cycle. Identify stages **A–F** by choosing from the options given below.

Testing **Design** **Analysis** **Feasibility Study** **Investigation** **Development**

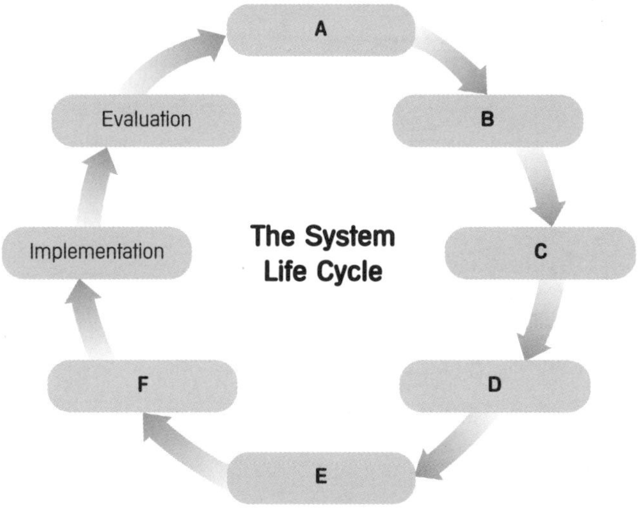

Stage	What Happens
A	
B	
C	
D	
E	
F	

7 When a new system is planned, an investigation is first carried out. Identify **three** methods that can be used in the investigation.

a) .... **b)** .... **c)** ....

8 Give **two** reasons why program maintenance might be necessary.

9 Which of the following is the output from the analysis stage of a project? Tick the correct option.

A A program ☐ **B** A requirements specification ☐
C A program design ☐ **D** A test plan ☐

10 Explain what is meant by beta testing.

Data and Information

Data and Information

1 What is the difference between data and information?

....

....

2 Which of the following statements about data are true? Tick the correct options.

- **A** Data can be symbols ☐
- **B** Data has no meaning ☐
- **C** Computers process data ☐
- **D** Meaningful output to a human from a computer is data ☐
- **E** Data tells you everything you need to know about an object ☐
- **F** Data can be stored on a hard disk ☐

3 Which of the following are examples of data? Tick the correct options.

Example	Tick or Cross
a) Bar code	
b) 11654587	
c) My birthday is 20/12/90	
d) 23-34-45	
e) 1101000011100000	
f) Diagnosis: swine flu	

4 Select the correct words from the options given to complete the following sentences.

output **context** **bits** **software** **meaning**

To a computer, data is a stream of .... with no .... What it means is determined by the .... and how it presents the .... to the user. The user has to have .... to make sense of the data.

Finding Information

1 Which of the following statements about finding information on the Internet are true? Tick the correct options.

- **A** Links can help you find more related information ☐
- **B** The information is always reliable ☐
- **C** The most up-to-date information appears at the top of the search list ☐
- **D** Information is often in multimedia format ☐
- **E** Information from university web sites is always reliable ☐
- **F** Information from governments is always reliable ☐

2 Select the correct words from the options given to complete the following sentences.

microblog **podcast** **wiki** **blog** **discussion board**

People can communicate and work together on the Internet. They can use a ………………………… to record what they do each day and people can comment on this. Small notes can be uploaded on a ………………………… .

People can cooperate on a piece of work by using a ………………………… or they can download a collection of files from a ………………………… to look at later. Many web sites provide a ………………………… where opinions can be posted.

3 Explain why printed information may often be more reliable than information posted online.

…………………………………………………………………………

…………………………………………………………………………

…………………………………………………………………………

4 How would you decide if a blog has information worth looking at?

…………………………………………………………………………

…………………………………………………………………………

…………………………………………………………………………

Document Processing

Presenting Information

1 Which of the following is a good reason for producing paper output from a computer? Tick the correct option.

- **A** Needed for legal reasons ☐
- **B** Takes less space than screen output ☐
- **C** Easier to store than screen output ☐
- **D** Uses less energy than screen output ☐

2 Match the following descriptions of word processing actions **1–5** to the correct answers **A–E**. Enter the appropriate numbers in the boxes provided.

1	Text is removed from one location and placed somewhere else
2	Text is duplicated to somewhere else
3	The setting that's accepted without being changed
4	Keep a copy of the file you are working on with a different name
5	Use the mouse to reposition text without using the menu or the keyboard

- **A** Save as ☐
- **B** Cut and paste ☐
- **C** Copy and paste ☐
- **D** Drag and drop ☐
- **E** Default ☐

Processors and Software

3 Select the correct words from the options given to complete the following sentences.

program code **text editor** **tables** **format** **program** **word processors** **bold**

If you just want to type in plain letters, you may want to use a .... These don't save special characters, which are needed to .... the document. If you are writing ...., these characters will stop the .... from working. .... add all sorts of extra data so that you can see effects such as .... or you can create .... that set out work more clearly.

Processors and Software (Cont.)

4 **a)** Explain why a writer might use the **track changes** option on a word processor.

....

....

b) What are **comments** used for in a word-processed document?

....

....

5 The following sentences all contain spelling mistakes. Which of them would always be picked up by a spell checker? Tick the correct options.

Sentence	Identified by Spell Checker?
a) Your my best friend.	☐
b) This is spelled rong.	☐
c) This is spelled rite.	☐
d) Their is a mistake here.	☐
e) I think u r wrong.	☐
f) There is an errror here.	☐

6 Select the correct words from the options given to complete the following sentences.

number **header** **gridlines** **footer** **table**

A .... is a standard piece of text that goes on the bottom of every page.

A .... goes on the top. They can be set to .... the pages automatically. A .... can be used to set text out in neat columns.

The .... in them let you see what you are doing more easily.

Graphics

Bit-mapped Graphics

1 Which of the following statements about bit-mapped graphics are true? Tick the correct options.

- **A** They represent pictures as pixels ☐
- **B** They can be enlarged without loss of quality ☐
- **C** The number of dots affects their resolution ☐
- **D** They use mathematical formulae to represent a picture ☐
- **E** They can't be compressed ☐
- **F** They take more storage space than an equivalent vector graphic ☐

2 Explain why bit-mapped graphics often have to be compressed before they're uploaded onto picture sharing web sites.

....

....

Imaging Software

3 Image A shows a flower. Image B shows part of the image enlarged.

Image A

Image B

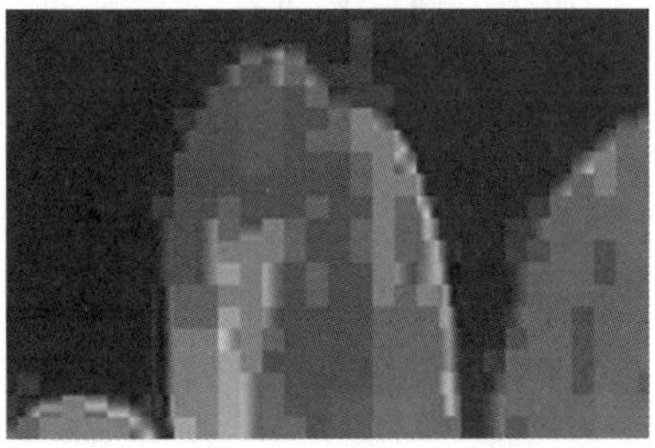

a) What type of image file is image A? ....

b) What has happened in the enlarging process to produce the unclear image B?

....

....

c) Which picture will take up more file space, image A or B?

....

Software for the Web

Viewing the Web

1. Select the correct words from the options given to complete the following sentences.

standard **browser** **web pages** **platform** **world wide web** **HTML**

The .... is made up from millions of .... They're all made up in a .... way, which means that they can be seen on any computer .... The coding system used is .... so any .... can display a web page on the computer where it's running.

Features Offered by Browsers

2. Which of the following are features offered by all web browsers? Tick the correct options.

A Search and replace ☐
B Cut and paste ☐
C A back button ☐
D Graphic editing ☐
E History ☐
F A URL box ☐

3. Why would someone need to use the **refresh** button on a web browser?

....

....

4. **a)** What is a URL?

....

b) What is the purpose of the URL box in a web browser?

....

5. What is the purpose of the **home** button on a browser?

....

....

Spreadsheets

Spreadsheets

1 A spreadsheet contains a reference **A1:B12**. What does this refer to? Tick the correct option.

A A cell ☐ **B** A row ☐ **C** A column ☐ **D** A range ☑

2 A spreadsheet contains a reference **=A1**. What does this refer to? Tick the correct option.

A A cell ☑ **B** A row ☐ **C** A column ☐ **D** A range ☐

Formulae, Functions, Cell Addressing and Formatting

3 Here are some entries in a spreadsheet with the formula view switched on. What values will be displayed in each of the cells B1 to B5? Write the answers in the boxes.

	A	B
1	12	=A1+A2
2	14	=A1/A4
3	25	=A4^A5
4	6	=(A1-A4)*A5
5	2	=SUM(A1:A5)

Cell Reference	Result Displayed
a) B1	26
b) B2	2
c) B3	36
d) B4	12
e) B5	59

4 Which of the following statements about spreadsheet functions are true? Tick the correct options.

A They have names ☑

B They're all concerned with calculations ☐

C They have brackets ☑

D They start with an equals sign ☑

E They produce a single value ☐

F They always contain a plus sign ☐

Formulae, Functions, Cell Addressing and Formatting (Cont.)

5 A spreadsheet contains the following expression in cell C10: **=IF(B10>=50, "PASS","FAIL")**

What will be displayed in cell C10 if B10 contains the following numbers?

a) 0: fail **b)** 49: fail **c)** 49.5: fail

d) 50: pass **e)** 51: pass

6 Cell B1 contains the expression **=A1+A2**, which is copied to cell C1.

Cell B2 contains the expression **=$A$2+$A$3**, which is copied to cell C2.

a) What formula will appear in C1? =B1 + B2

b) What formula will appear in C2? = $A$2 + $A$3

c) Explain what has happened. The $ sign makes sure that the formula does not change (absolute reference)

7 What are pivot tables used for?

Graphs

8 Circle the correct options in the following sentences.

To produce a chart, the data that's needed is **selected** / **deselected** and if necessary, the **headings** / **footers** are also included. You then select the chart **witch** / **wizard** which asks some questions and then **automates** / **suspends** the chart-making process. If you want to show values as a proportion of the whole, you will use a **pie** / **circle** chart. A trend is often shown better as a **line** / **cross** or a **bar** / **pub** chart.

9 Outline the steps you would take to produce a simple macro for a spreadsheet.

You must write in macro language

Presentations

What are Presentations?

1 Which of the following are uses of presentation software? Tick the correct options.

- **A** To make a public display of information ☐
- **B** To make a slide show ☑
- **C** To make a web page ☐
- **D** To make a flyer ☐
- **E** To show a set of photographs ☑
- **F** To illustrate a lesson ☑

Multimedia

2 List the forms of information that might be part of a multimedia display.

Pictures, videos, text

3 Which of the following are common advantages of using a multimedia presentation over the printed page? Tick the correct options.

- **A** It often engages people's attention more ☑
- **B** It contains better presented material ☑
- **C** It's quicker to produce ☐
- **D** It's easier to keep up to date ☐
- **E** It doesn't depend on the skills of the speaker ☑
- **F** People always enjoy a presentation ☑

Presentation Software

4 How does a template help to quickly produce a presentation?

don't customise yourself

Presentation Software (Cont.)

5 Select the correct words from the options given to complete the following sentences.

movie clips **transitions** **handouts** **animations**

A presentation can be made more interesting if you use .... These are the special effects that happen when you move from one slide to the next. .... can be used to move individual words into place as the audience watches. .... can be added to show real-life events. .... should be produced so that the audience can take away information from the meeting.

Good Design

6 Select the correct words from the options given to complete the following sentences.

consistent **master slide** **limited** **logo** **few**

Unless some thought is given to a presentation, it could end up being boring. To make a presentation easy to follow, the number of colours should be .... and there should only be a ....few........ bullet points on each slide.

It's important that each slide is .... so it seems to belong to the set. This can be achieved by placing common information like a .... on a ....

7 Here is a slide from a presentation.

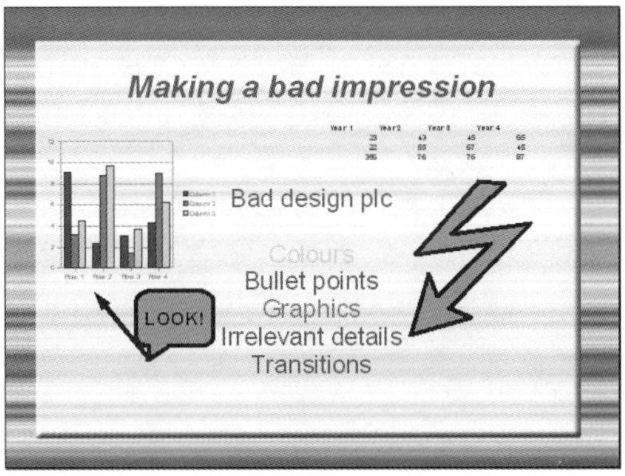

Make a list of the bad design points on this slide.

have to understand whats happening

Arrows wonky, too many colours

Databases

Databases

1. Which of the following applications require databases? Tick the correct options.

   A Online shopping ☐

   B Running a supermarket loyalty card scheme ☐

   C Controlling a microwave oven ☐

   D Supporting a mobile phone network ☐

   E A burglar alarm system ☐

   F Online banking ☐

Flat File and Relational Databases

2. Select the correct words from the options given to complete the following sentences.

   field **organised** **spreadsheet** **record** **flat file**

   A database is a store of information that is .... so that it can easily be processed. A simple database consists only of rows and columns of data and this is called a .... database.

   Each row is a .... and each column is a ....

   Databases like this aren't very flexible, but they can easily be set up using .... software although this is rarely a good idea.

3. **a)** What is meant by data redundancy?

   ....

   b) Why can data redundancy be a problem?

   ....

Flat File and Relational Databases (Cont.)

4 Here is the structure of a relational database. Complete the table below.

Question	Answer
a) The number of entities represented	
b) Identify four primary key fields	
c) The foreign key in tbl property	
d) The number of links	
e) The data type for gender in tbl landlord	

5 **a)** What is the purpose of a key field? ....

b) Choosing from the options given below, identify a suitable key field for the sets of data in the table.

car colour **car make** **account holder's name** **student's name**

author's name **captain's name** **enrolment number** **car registration** **book title**

International Standard Book Number **flight number** **account number**

Data Set	Suitable Key Field
i) Flights from an airport	
ii) Used cars in a showroom	
iii) Bank accounts	
iv) Students in a college	
v) Books in a book shop	

Flat File and Relational Databases (Cont.)

6 Match the database objects **1–4** with their purpose **A–H**. Some items are used more than once.

A	To produce a printed list
B	To select a subset of records
C	To link tables
D	To store data about an entity
E	To present data in some order
F	To summarise a set of data
G	To present data on the screen
H	To make it easy to enter data on the screen

Database Object

1 Table ....

2 Report ....

3 Query ....

4 Form ....

Database Software

7 Choosing from the three options given, identify the software responsible for the following purposes in a database. (Items of software may be used more than once.)

A DBMS **B Wizard** **C Application**

Purpose	Type of Software
a) Creating a data structure	....
b) Processing a library record system	....
c) Setting up a table	....
d) Finding all customers who are late paying	....
e) Choosing a report to run	....
f) Finding data from its location on the disk	....

Databases

Data Types

8 Match the data types in the table with the following descriptions.

A Whole numbers

B Fractional numbers

C Yes or No, True or False

D Letters only

E An extensive piece of writing

F A sum of money

Data Type	Description
a) Currency	
b) Integer	
c) Floating point	
d) Text	
e) Boolean	
f) Alphabetic	

Querying a Database

9 **a)** Here is a query applied to a relational database about employees in a company.

PRINT surname, telephone_number, salary WHERE salary>=30000 AND date_appointed<20/12/10

Explain what it's intended to do.

b) Here is a similar query applied to the same database.

PRINT surname, telephone_number, salary WHERE salary>=30000 OR date_appointed<20/12/10

Which query, **a)** or **b)** would be likely to generate the longer list? Explain why.

Data Capture

What is Data Capture?

1. Explain why automated data capture is generally preferable to human data entry.

Forms

2. The paper form below is given to applicants for a job. Give **five** reasons why this is a poorly designed form.

Job application form

Name................................

DOB................................

Qualifications....................

....

Address..............................

....

Phone................................

Email................................

Position applied for...........

Salary expected.................

3. Below are some controls used on screen forms to capture data. Identify each one and explain how it's used.

Control	Type of Control	How it is Used
a) 	i)	ii)
b) 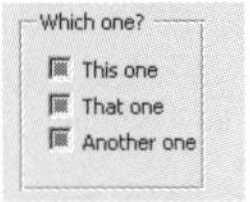	i)	ii)
c) 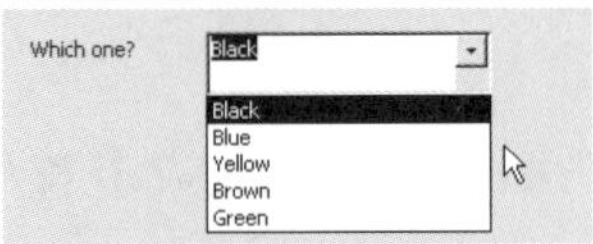	i)	ii)
d) 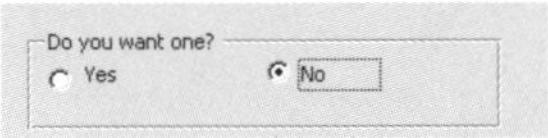	i)	ii)
e) 	i)	ii)

Validation and Verification

1 For each of the data items below, suggest and describe a suitable validation method.

Data Item	Validation Method
a) Date of birth of a job applicant	
b) Number of doors on a car	
c) Gender of a job applicant	
d) Barcode of an item in a shop	
e) Surname	
f) Telephone	

2 Select the correct words from the options given to complete the following sentences.

re-entered **differences** **computer** **original** **mistakes**

Verification can be carried out by getting two operators to enter the same data. The .... then checks the two versions for any .... If there are any, then .... must have been made and the data is .... Alternatively, a document can be read on screen and compared with the .... to see if there are any problems.

Automated Data Entry

3 Identify **three** methods of automatic data entry used at a supermarket checkout.

4 Explain why voice recognition is a difficult technology to implement for data input.

Computer Control

Controlling Devices and Feedback

1. Select the correct words from the options given to complete the following sentences.

acceleration **feedback** **actuator** **cruise control** **limit** **sensor**

Computers make use of .... in order to keep a condition constant. For example, a car's .... can be set to a certain speed. A .... detects the speed of the car and if it drops below the desired ...., more .... is applied by an .... which delivers more fuel to the engine.

2. Match the descriptions **1–5** to the correct answers **A–E**. Enter the appropriate numbers in the boxes provided.

1	A computer system that flies a plane
2	Continuously variable data from the real world
3	The type of data that computers handle
4	A device that detects physical changes and produces signals
5	A type of control system that acts to keep a variable within limits

A Feedback loop ☐

B Autopilot ☐

C Digital ☐

D Analogue ☐

E Sensor ☐

Robots and Control Programming

3. What is a robot?

....

....

Data Logging

1 Why is computer data logging usually preferred to taking readings manually?

....

....

....

2 Here are some activities that require data logging. For each one, identify the sensor that would be required.

Example of Data Logging	Sensor Required
Odometer (mileage recording in a car)	a) ....
Traffic passing a point in the road	b) ....
Number of people going through a door	c) ....
The performance of an industrial oven	d) ....
The dampness in the air in a greenhouse	e) ....

3 What would be suitable sampling intervals when logging the following activities? Choose from the options given.

1 tenth of a second **100th of a millisecond** **1 hour** **1 second** **1 minute**

Situation	Suitable Interval
The speed of a car	a) ....
The temperature of the air over a year	b) ....
The temperature of an oven when baking a cake	c) ....
The intensity of light from a photographic flash	d) ....
Use of a mobile telephone for billing purposes	e) ....

Telemetry and Visualisation

4 Explain why logged data is often visualised by the computer as charts or other displays.

....

....

Files and Compression

Files

1. Define the term **computer file**.

....

Structured and Unstructured Files

2. Select the correct words from the options given to complete the following sentences.

word processor **records** **binary** **relational database** **bits**

Structured files are often organised into .... In a ...., these are all the same size. .... files aren't organised predictably. For example, a letter written using a .... can have anything in it in any order. Similarly, the sequence of .... in a music file can be unpredictable.

3. Select the correct words from the options given to complete the following sentences.

letters **stored** **type** **dates** **doc**

File names should be chosen so that it's clear what is being .... Reference numbers and .... are helpful so that you can find the right file immediately. Most files are stored with an extension. This is a set of extra .... that shows what .... of file it is. For example, ... after a file name usually means that it's a word-processed document.

4. State **two** reasons why most operating systems add extensions to file names.

....

....

Files and Compression

Structured and Unstructured Files (Cont.)

5 Identify the type of file associated with the following extensions.

Extension	Type of File	Extension	Type of File
HTML	a)	zip	e)
pdf	b)	MP3	f)
txt	c)	JPEG	g)
doc	d)		

Compression

6 State **two** reasons why files might need to be compressed.

7 State **two** disadvantages of compressing files.

Lossy and Lossless Compression

8 The following statements are about compression. Tick whether each one is true or false.

Statement	True	False
a) Files compressed by a lossy method can't be recovered in their original form		
b) Usually more space is saved when using lossy file compression than when using lossless methods		
c) MP3 is a lossless file compression method		
d) JPEG is a lossless file compression method		
e) JPEG is used for image files		
f) A compressed file uses fewer bits than its uncompressed equivalent		

Security

Security Issues and Backing up

1 What is a backup?

2 Which of the following are good places to store backed up and sensitive data from a big organisation? Tick the correct options.

A Online

B Off-site storage facility

C With the server

D In the data centre

E At home

F In a cupboard in the office

3 Which of these are reasons to backup data? Tick the correct options.

A Data may get corrupted

B Data may get erased

C Data may be copied illegally

D Data may be inaccurate

E Data may not be up to date

F Data may have been incorrectly updated

4 Which of the following are carried out when data is archived? Tick the correct options.

A Data is copied

B Data is updated

C Data is amended

D Data is erased

E Data is stored

F Data is validated

5 How often should data be backed up? Tick the correct option.

A Every day

B Every time it changes

C Often enough so that an up-to-date copy can be re-created

D Whenever you get the time

Network Security

1. Select the correct words from the options given to complete the following sentences.

user ID **users** **privileges** **directories** **log in**

In a network, many .... could have access to data. It's therefore important that they have sufficient .... to be able to do their work, but not so many that they can access irrelevant data.

Users identify themselves with a .... when they .... so that they gain access to the correct ...., which contain the files they need.

2. What is meant by a **strong** password?

3. Give **three** pieces of advice on how you would choose a strong password.

4. State **three** easy methods that hackers can use to find out someone's password.

5. Describe how biometrics can be helpful in keeping data safe.

Online Security

Hackers and Hacking Software

1. Which of the following statements about computer viruses are true? Tick the correct options.

   A They always cause damage ☐
   B They can damage your hardware ☐
   C They are programs ☐
   D They copy themselves ☐
   E They can sometimes carry a payload ☐
   F They can arrive as email attachments ☐

2. Select the correct words from the options given to complete the following sentences.

   software **browser** **virus** **web site** **advertisements** **spam**

   Hackers may try to access your PC so that they can use it to send .... to lots of other people. They may also take control of your .... so that it displays a .... chosen by the hacker instead of the one you want.

   Often, pop-up .... are displayed, which try to frighten you into believing that you have a .... and that you need to buy special .... to remove it.

3. Circle the correct word in each of the following sentences.

   a) Unwanted mail is **spam / malware**.
   b) A virus that spreads through a network is called a **worm / Trojan**.
   c) The part of a virus that can cause damage to data is called its **signature / payload**.
   d) One type of software that detects your passwords is a **keylogger / worm**.
   e) Taking control of your browser is called **hacking / hijacking**.

4. Which of the following are examples of malware? Tick the correct options.

   A A virus ☐ **B** A cookie ☐
   C A browser history ☐ **D** A browser cache file ☐
   E A Trojan horse ☐ **F** A pop-up ☐

Data Transfer

1 Select the correct words from the options given to complete the following sentences.

routes **transmitted** **encrypt** **wireless** **received** **intercepted** **packets**

In most networks, data is divided into units called .... before being .... These are sent by different .... and reassembled when .... They can be .... and examined and the information can then be misused. This misuse is particularly easy on .... networks and so it's wise to .... the data before sending it so that anyone who sees it will not be able to read it.

Precautions

2 Circle the correct word in each of the following sentences.

a) Encrypted mail is **scrambled / hidden**.

b) To read encrypted mail you need to have a **key / password**.

c) Companies often prohibit staff from bringing in memory sticks because they could **lose them / introduce a virus.**

d) A firewall can examine your **hard disk / data packets**.

e) A firewall can reduce the risk of **hacking / making data entry errors**.

3 Which of the following are good policies for a company to adopt in order to reduce the risk of a virus infection? Tick the correct options.

A Ban the use of emails ☐

B Prevent access to programs attached to emails ☐

C Forbid the use of memory sticks ☐

D Scan incoming files ☐

E Scan outgoing files ☐

F Monitor employees' keystrokes ☐

The Internet

What is the Internet?

1 Which of the following statements about the Internet are true? Tick the correct options.

- **A** It's the same thing as the world wide web ☐
- **B** It's a network of networks ☐
- **C** It uses a common set of protocols ☐
- **D** It's run by a central organisation ☐
- **E** It wouldn't function without HTML ☐
- **F** It's owned by a consortium of companies ☐

2 Circle the correct word in each of the following sentences.

a) The Internet is **an infrastructure / a set of services**.

b) The rules that control the transmission of information on the Internet are **standardised / variable**.

c) You can connect to the Internet by having an account with **an internet service provider / a search engine**.

d) Internet service providers normally provide **a cable to your home / email**.

e) Web pages are written in **HTML / HTTP**.

World Wide Web

3 Select the correct words from the options given to complete the following sentences.

web sites **links** **web browser** **web pages** **page** **hypertext**

The world wide web is a collection of ...., which are grouped as .... They're accessed and displayed on your computer by software called a .... They make use of ...., which is special text that contains .... to other locations on the same .... or on a different site.

4 Which of the following are protocols used on the Internet? Tick the correct options.

A HTML ☐	**B** HTTP ☐
C TCP ☐	**D** PDF ☐
E IP ☐	**F** JPEG ☐

5 What is an HTML **tag** as used in web pages?

....

The Internet and Online Safety

Search Engines

1 Select the correct words from the options given to complete the following sentences.

advertising **search engine** **catalogue** **links** **clicked** **database**

An online tool that helps you to find what you want on the world wide web is called a

.... They .... web sites into a ....

They make most of their money by .... , in some cases getting a fee every time a

link is .... The Page Rank system categorises sites according to the number of

.... there are from other sites.

Other Services from Search Engines

2 Explain why a search engine might provide an email service free of charge.

....

....

3 Make a list of **five** other services provided by search engine web sites.

....

....

....

New Dangers, Chat and Social Networking

4 Make a list of **four** precautions that you should take when chatting online.

....

....

5 Give **four** precautions you should take when setting yourself up on a social networking site.

....

....

Online Safety

Phishing and Other Scams

1 Which of the following are possible consequences of phishing? Tick the correct options.

- **A** Identity theft ☐
- **B** Theft from your bank account ☐
- **C** Your computer might contract a virus ☐
- **D** Your computer might run slowly ☐
- **E** Someone might open a bank account in your name ☐
- **F** Files may get deleted from your computer ☐

2 Here is an email received from an unknown sender.

E-mail

Delete | Reply | Forward | Spam

International Promotion / Prize Award Dept.
From: Microware Corporation Email Lottery International
World Internet Lotto Center
Western Avenue 4712

We hereby bring to your notice that a consignment been delivered at your residence by two diplomats. They had been stopped by us. There is a security measure put in place by United States of America, check terrorism and money laundry through the sale of illegal drugs locally and internationally.

After examination, we found out that the consignment contained the sum of US$5.7 Million, which upon further investigation revealed that the fund was your inheritance.

Consequently, the diplomats will deliver your consignment at your residence after all protocols have been observed.

However, in order to proceed we need you to reconfirm the following information,

Full Name: ....

Residential Address:....

Date of Birth: ....

Occupation: ....

Telephone/Mobile Numbers: ....

We await your response.

Regards,

Jason Ahern.

Make a list of **four** reasons why this email is clearly a scam.

....

....

....

Online Services

1. Which of the following are advantages of shopping online? Tick the correct options.

- **A** There's a wider choice of goods ☐
- **B** Better quality goods ☐
- **C** You get your goods more quickly ☐
- **D** You can always trust the vendor to deliver ☐
- **E** You can more easily find the best deal ☐
- **F** Goods are cheaper ☐

2. Which of the following statements about reading the news online are true? Tick the correct options.

- **A** It's more likely to be up to date than in a newspaper ☐
- **B** It's more likely to be unbiased than in a newspaper ☐
- **C** It's more likely to be in depth than in a newspaper ☐
- **D** It may be in multimedia format ☐
- **E** It's easier to find related stories than in a newspaper ☐
- **F** It's not cluttered by advertisements ☐

3. Give two advantages and two disadvantages of studying online. Write your answers in the boxes.

Advantages	Disadvantages

4. Give two advantages and two disadvantages of using online services to translate text into another language. Write your answers in the boxes.

Advantages	Disadvantages

Communications

Personal Communications

1 Which of the following statements about web-based email are true? Tick the correct options.

- **A** It provides exactly the same services as client-based email ☐
- **B** It can be accessed from any Internet connected computer ☐
- **C** It doesn't impose file size limits ☐
- **D** It doesn't provide virus scanning ☐
- **E** It often provides spam filters ☐
- **F** It provides an address book of contacts ☐

Email

2 Here is a screen for creating an email.

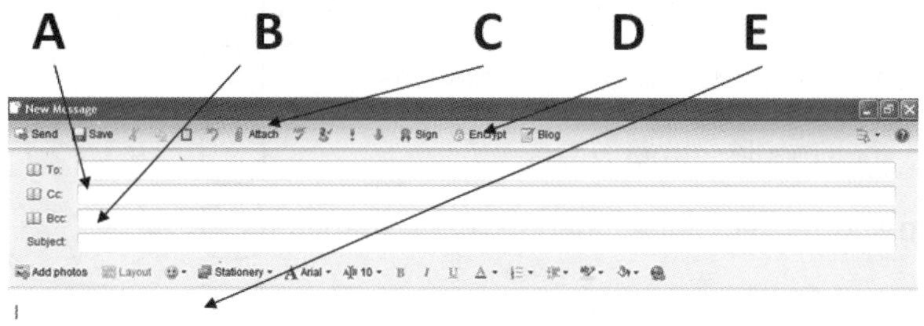

Identify the part of the screen used for the following actions.

a) You write the message ....

b) You make it impossible for someone else to read ....

c) You copy it to someone else but without anyone else knowing ....

d) You copy it to someone else ....

e) You send a spreadsheet file ....

Other Communication Methods

3 Which of the following statements about VoIP are true? Tick the correct options.

- **A** It relies on packet switching ☐
- **B** It's an analogue method of communication ☐
- **C** It can be free ☐
- **D** It can be less reliable than traditional telephone calls ☐
- **E** It's good for making emergency calls ☐
- **F** It's secure against eavesdropping ☐

Other Communication Methods (Cont.)

4 Which of the following statements about Internet chatting are true? Tick the correct options.

- **A** It's always one-to-one ☐
- **B** It can be used for business conferences ☐
- **C** It allows the sending of files ☐
- **D** It is text only ☐
- **E** It makes use of Internet protocol ☐
- **F** It's totally private ☐

5 Blogs and microblogs are common ways of communicating.

Tick whether each statement refers to blogs and/or microblogs.

Statement	Blog	Microblog
a) Available on a web site	☐	☐
b) Often sent from a mobile phone	☐	☐
c) Very short messages	☐	☐
d) Allows feedback from readers	☐	☐
e) Useful for real-time news updates	☐	☐

Impact on Society

6 What does it mean when a web posting **goes viral**?

....

....

7 Give **three** reasons why it might be a bad idea to spend a lot of time on social networking sites.

....

....

....

Entertainment

Bookings

1 **a)** State **two** ways that online services can help when making a theatre or concert booking.

....

....

b) State **two** ways that online services can help when making hotel bookings.

....

....

Streaming

2 Select the correct words from the options given to complete the following sentences.

RAM **download** **streaming** **MP3 player** **processor** **buffer**

You can .... music files and play them on your ....

Some services play the music as it arrives, a process called .... This needs the data to be run into a part of .... called a .... , which then sends the data on to the .... for decoding.

Music Downloads and Gaming

3 Match the following descriptions of actions **1–5** to the correct answers **A–E**. Enter the appropriate numbers in the boxes provided.

	Action
1	A way of sharing files without the need for a web server
2	The act of copying data from a remote server to your PC
3	The act of copying data from your PC to a remote server
4	The status of a file that prohibits you making copies of it
5	A browser plug-in that lets you play animations in web pages

A Flash ☐
B Uploading ☐
C Peer-to-peer ☐
D Downloading ☐
E Copyright ☐

Computer Crime

1. Select the correct words from the options given to complete the following sentences.

characters **access** **brute force** **copy** **passwords**

Hackers attempt to gain unauthorised .... to computer systems. Often they do this so that they can .... data and make use of it.

They can get hold of .... by asking users for them or by using .... techniques to try every available combination of letters, numbers and ....

2. Match the descriptions **1–5** to the correct answers **A–E**. Enter the appropriate numbers in the boxes provided.

	Action
1	A branch of computer science that attempts to find evidence of computer crime
2	The misuse of computer access in order to discover industrial secrets
3	Unsolicited email
4	Software designed to block unsolicited email
5	The unlawful use of someone else's personal information for personal gain

A Espionage ☐
B Forensics ☐
C Spam ☐
D Identity theft ☐
E Filter ☐

3. Select the correct words from the options given to complete the following sentences.

servers **bandwidth** **hard disks** **address list** **reply**

Spam can cost an organisation a lot because it uses up ...., which should be carrying work-related data. It also takes up space on the .... of the .... The worst of it can be blocked, but that runs the risk of blocking legitimate emails as well.

One of the most important ways to control spam is never to .... to it. Individuals can reduce the problem by only allowing email from those on their ....

Legal Matters

Laws

1 Which of the following are provisions of the UK Data Protection Act (1998)? Tick the correct options.

- **A** Data mustn't be sent outside the country ☐
- **B** Personal data mustn't be collected by unlawful means ☐
- **C** Personal data can't be used for statistical purposes ☐
- **D** Personal data must be accurate ☐
- **E** Personal data should be adequately protected ☐
- **F** No third party shall ever be allowed to see personal data ☐

2 Match the descriptions **1–5** to the correct answers **A–E**. Enter the appropriate numbers in the boxes provided.

	Action
1	The person entrusted in the UK to oversee data protection issues
2	A person about whom personal data is stored on a computer system
3	A person who holds personal data about others
4	An example of personal data
5	A provision of the Data Protection Act

- **A** Right of access ☐
- **B** Information Commissioner ☐
- **C** Address ☐
- **D** Data subject ☐
- **E** Data controller ☐

3 Give **three** reasons why a Data Protection Act is considered necessary.

....

....

....

4 State the name of the UK law that's intended to criminalise hacking.

....

Disability and Visual Impairment

1 Which of the following are ways in which people with a visual impairment can be helped to use a computer system? Tick the correct options.

A Braille printers ☐ **B** Voice output ☐

C Change screen colours ☐ **D** Sticky keys ☐

E Alter mouse sensitivity ☐ **F** Make a sound when a feature is turned on ☐

Access to Computers and Internet

2 Which of the following are likely to increase the use of online services? Tick the correct options.

A Provide broadband more widely ☐

B Increase bandwidth generally ☐

C Better education ☐

D Increase taxes ☐

E Provide incentives for communications companies to improve infrastructure ☐

F Allow market forces to provide what's wanted ☐

Health and Safety

3 Here are some examples of advice given for safety and comfort when working with a computer.

For each one, state one benefit of following the advice.

Advice	Benefit
Take frequent breaks	**a)**
Install air conditioning	**b)**
Reduce back lighting	**c)**
Protect all cables	**d)**
Don't drink at the keyboard	**e)**

Modern Work Issues

Impact of IT on Work

1 Which of the following is a result of the widespread use of IT in the workplace? Tick the correct options.

- **A** Less work is done ☐
- **B** People work fewer hours ☐
- **C** People work more from home ☐
- **D** Less paper is used ☐
- **E** People can work on the move more easily ☐
- **F** It becomes difficult to switch off from work ☐

Collaborative Working

2 Which of the following can help people to work effectively together? Tick the correct options.

- **A** Video conferencing ☐
- **B** VoIP ☐
- **C** Cloud computing ☐
- **D** Home working ☐
- **E** LANs ☐
- **F** The 'track changes' feature of a word processor ☐

Software as a Service

3 Which of the following are advantages of using Software as a Service? Tick the correct options.

- **A** Removes the responsibility to upgrade software ☐
- **B** No need to make arrangements for backup ☐
- **C** Easier to set standards ☐
- **D** Quality of work improves ☐
- **E** Removes the need for LANs ☐
- **F** Removes the need to track software licences ☐

Working with IT Systems

Getting the Best from PCs

1. What is an **intuitive** system?

....

2. Give one advantage and one disadvantage of accepting the default settings for a word processor.

....

Starting Up and Shutting Down

3. What is meant by booting up a computer? ....

4. Select the correct words from the options given to complete the following sentences.

desktop **profile** **colour scheme** **utilities** **browser**

When a computer system has many users, each one may be given a ....

This stores details such as which .... you prefer for accessing web pages, or

which .... you like best on the .... There are many

.... that allow you to set the features that you want.

Maintenance and Running the Computer

5. Here is the folder organisation that a student set up. State **five** bad decisions that were made in choosing this structure.

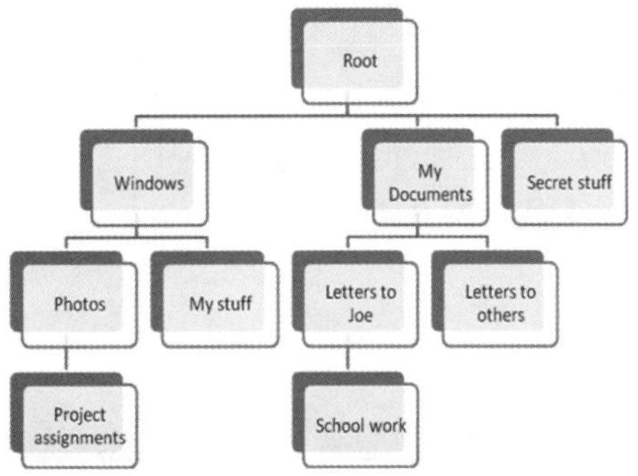

....

....

....

....

....

6. Describe **two** ways that you can speed up a computer that has started to run more slowly than it used to.

....

....

Exam-style Questions

1 A veterinary practice has a database of the animals that it treats. Part of the database is shown below.

Animal_ID	Animal_type	Animal_name	Animal_DOB	Vaccinated	Sex	Owner_forename	Owner_surname
100	snake	Tiger	26/07/2004	YES	m	David	Calhoun
101	gerbil	Buster	10/07/1993	YES	m	Noah	Jimenez
102	cat	George	03/02/1991	YES	f	Amir	Torres
103	hamster	Jack	29/08/1997	NO	f	Eaton	Carr
104	rabbit	Jack	10/07/1992	NO	m	Aurora	Haynes
105	gerbil	Sid	12/07/2010	YES	f	Lara	Harrell
107	budgie	Jack	29/09/2000	NO	m	Ava	Ray
108	rabbit	Martha	09/03/2003	YES	f	Kendall	Fischer
109	snake	Daisy	27/07/2004	NO	f	Gillian	Blackburn
110	cat	Henry	15/02/2006	YES	m	Ori	Gilbert
111	dog	Hobo	21/01/2006	NO	f	Colby	Christian
113	spider	George	10/08/2002	NO	f	Shaeleigh	Tanner
114	horse	Josh	06/05/2007	NO	m	Regina	Trevino
115	snake	Sid	22/01/2007	NO	f	Madeline	Carver
116	rabbit	Tiger	26/08/1996	NO	f	Orlando	Montgomery
117	spider	Buster	28/01/1998	YES	m	Sylvia	Dickson
118	horse	Nellie	26/08/1997	NO	m	Rajah	Graves
119	horse	Badger	05/09/2009	YES	f	Simone	Davenport
120	rabbit	Hobo	13/06/2004	NO	f	Igor	Chandler

a) How many records are shown here? ....

b) Fill in the table to identify the data type used for each of the following fields.

Field Name	Data Type
Animal_ID	**i)** ....
Animal_type	**ii)** ....
Animal_DOB (date of birth)	**iii)** ....
Vaccinated	**iv)** ....
Sex	**v)** ....

c) Which field is the only one suitable as a key field? ....

d) The vet's receptionist runs the following query:

PRINT Animal_type, Animal_name, Animal_DOB WHERE Animal_DOB<01/01/2000 AND Vaccinated="NO"

With reference from the database, show the output that would result from this query.

e) Write a query that would find the surnames of all the owners whose animals were born on or after 1st January 2009.

f) **i)** The vet wants to store details of the treatments that each animal receives. Explain why a new table is needed to do this.

ii) State the fields that would be needed in this new table.

g) The animal database is set up using forms to make it easier to use. The following form is used for entering and displaying the animal information.

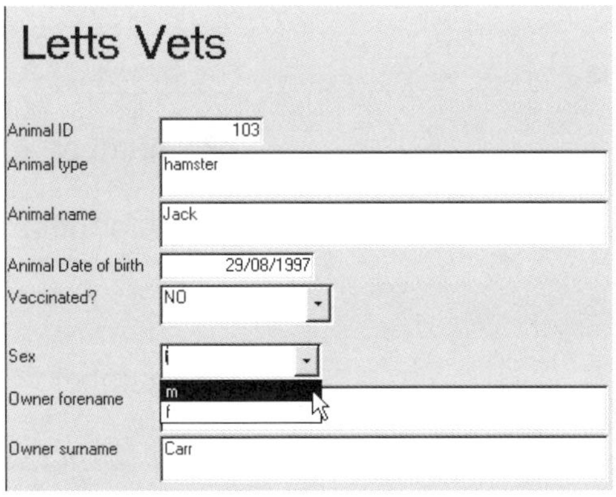

i) Explain what is meant by **validation**.

ii) Explain how the sex field is validated in this example.

h) The 'Animal Date of Birth' field is wrong – hamsters usually only live about 2 years. Explain how validation could have prevented this mistake.

Exam-style Questions

2 A teacher has recorded in a spreadsheet the marks scored by his class in some recent exam papers. There are three exam papers, each one marked out of 100.

The spreadsheet has been set up to calculate the totals and averages and also to look up the grades.

	A	B	C	D	E	F	G	H	I
1	**First Name**	**Surname**	**Mark 1**	**Mark 2**	**Mark 3**	**Total**	**Percentage**	**Grade**	**Pass/fail**
2	Rajah	Graves	24	30	34	89	30	F	FAIL
3	Simone	Davenport	43	44	68	154	51	C	PASS
4	Igor	Chandler	39	52	9	100	33	E	FAIL
5	Galvin	Powers	72	25	16	113	38	E	FAIL
6	Shea	Maxwell	30	85	20	135	45	D	FAIL
7	Tanya	Stewart	21	97	83	202	67	B	PASS
8	Phelan	Hewitt	87	67	79	233	78	A	PASS
9	Blake	Chang	56	43	49	148	49	D	FAIL
10	Jamalia	Buchanan	10	78	51	139	46	D	FAIL
11	Jorden	Golden	78	40	56	173	58	C	PASS
12	Brock	Holder	35	91	27	153	51	C	PASS
13	Sasha	Morrison	52	57	9	118	39	E	FAIL
14	**Average**		**46**	**59**	**42**	**146**	**49**		
15									
16	**Grade boundaries**								
17	**Lowest mark for grade**	**Grade**							
18	10	U							
19	20	F							
20	30	E							
21	40	D							
22	50	C							
23	60	B							
24	75	A							

a) The content of cell A18 is...

A text ◯ **B** number ◯

C a function ◯ **D** a formula ◯

b) The content of cell C14 is...

A text ◯ **B** number ◯

C a function ◯ **D** a formula ◯

c) The cell H2 contains =VLOOKUP(G2,$A$18:$B$24,2). This is a...

A value ◯ **B** function ◯

C formula ◯ **D** calculation ◯

d) The content of cell I2 is worked out automatically. It contains...

A =IF(G2>=50,"PASS","FAIL") ◯ **B** =IF(G2>=50,"FAIL","PASS") ◯

C =IF(G2<=50,"PASS","FAIL") ◯ **D** =IF(G2=50,"PASS","FAIL") ◯

e) Which of these would give the correct result in cell G7?

A =F6/300*100 ◯ **B** =F7/100 ◯

C =F7/300*100 ◯ **D** =F7/300 ◯

f) The cell H2 contains =VLOOKUP(G2,$A$18:$B$24,2).

This expression contains absolute cell references.

i) Identify the absolute cell references.

....

ii) Explain the meaning of an absolute cell reference.

....

....

g) The following graph shows the percentages obtained by the students.

i) Explain how this graph is produced.

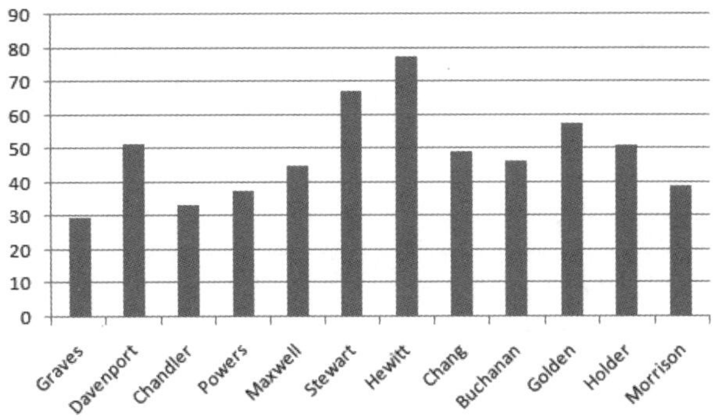

....

....

....

....

ii) Describe **two** ways that this graph can be imported into a word-processed report.

....

....

....

....

h) The cell F2 contains the expression =SUM(C2:E2). Describe the steps that can be taken to enter this into the cell without typing.

....

....

Exam-style Questions

3 A programming language has the following commands to draw shapes with a pen.

Command Example	Meaning
BK 50	Back 50 steps
FD 50	Forward 50 steps
LT 90	Left 90 degrees
PD	Pen Down (start writing)
PU	Pen Up (stop writing)
RT	Right 90 degrees

Example: (The small triangle represents the pen.)

Command List	**Drawing**
PD	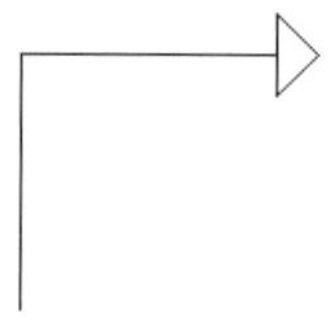
FD 100	
RT 90	
FD 100	
PU	

a) Write a set of commands that will draw the following shape with the same height as the example above.

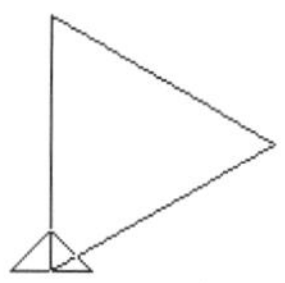

b) The programming language allows you to repeat commands to save you typing everything out. For example, you can draw a square by typing REPEAT 4 [FD 100 RT 90].

i) Draw the shape that would be produced by the following command:

PD REPEAT 6 [FD 50 RT 360/6] PU

ii) Write a set of commands that would produce a large letter 'T' like this:

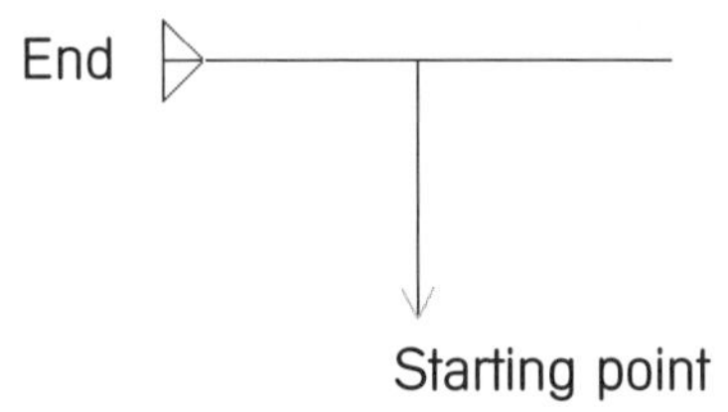

Exam-style Questions

4 **a)** Describe **three** services provided by a social networking site.

....

....

....

b) Explain why employers often look up details of job applicants on social networking sites.

....

....

....

c) Give **three** reasons why the police might look at social networking sites.

....

....

....

d) Explain how you can prevent people looking at your details when you don't want them to.

....

....

....

e) Describe how using a social networking site can be a useful way to make new friends.

....

....

....

....

f) Security is important when using a social networking site. You should choose a strong password so that others can't easily guess it.

Describe **three** ways that a password can be made strong.

....

....

....

g) Some social networking sites store cookies on your computer. Describe what a cookie is.

....

....

h) State **two** reasons why some people want to disable cookies on their computers.

....

....

5 Many electronic items in the home now contain microprocessors. Discuss, in as much detail as you can, the impact that these microprocessors have had.

6 Henry is a salesman who travels internationally. He often needs to log into his company's network in order to check stock availability and prices. He also has to communicate with his head office as well as with clients while on the move. He carries with him a PDA and a notebook computer.

a) What is a PDA?

b) Describe **three** work-related uses that Henry would have for his PDA while travelling.

c) When waiting for his plane at an airport, Henry often wants to connect his notebook computer to the Internet. He can use a WiFi hotspot or a mobile broadband service.

i) Describe what is meant by WiFi.

ii) Describe what is meant by a WiFi hotspot.

d) Henry notices that the WiFi connection at different airports is sometimes too slow to be very useful.

i) Explain **two** reasons why a WiFi connection may be slow.

ii) The WiFi provided at the airport is **open** and **unencrypted**. Explain what this means.

e) Henry's company has a strict policy that travelling staff must not use unencrypted WiFi connections for sending or receiving company data. Explain the reason for this policy.

f) At home, Henry has his own wireless network. Explain what each of the following are and how they can be used to help keep his home connection secure.

i) WEP

ii) MAC address

iii) SSID

iv) Sometimes, when he is travelling, Henry uses his mobile broadband connection to access the Internet. Describe **two** advantages and **two** disadvantages of using this instead of a WiFi hotspot.

g) Henry sometimes uses a Bluetooth connection.

i) Explain what Bluetooth is.

ii) Explain why Henry would sometimes want to use Bluetooth.

iii) Henry often uses VoIP in order to contact clients. Explain what VoIP is.

iv) Describe **two** benefits and **two** drawbacks of using VoIP to contact a client.

Exam-style Questions

7 Charlotte is using her home PC to access the Internet. She uses a browser and an email client. Her PC has the protocol TCP/IP installed on it.

a) Explain what a browser is.

b) Some browsers are **open source**. Explain what is meant by the term open source.

c) Explain why some users have open source browsers.

d) Explain what is meant by the term **proprietary software**.

e) Explain why many companies use proprietary software instead of open source.

f) Explain what is meant by a protocol.

g) Explain what TCP/IP is.

h) Charlotte has a broadband connection. Explain what a broadband connection is.

i) Charlotte often downloads music and video files. Explain why a broadband connection is necessary for this.

j) The music files that Charlotte downloads are in a compressed MP3 format. Explain what a compressed file is.

k) MP3 is a lossy form of compression. Explain what lossy compression is.

l) Explain why lossy MP3 files are generally considered an acceptable standard.

m) Charlotte often sends 'tweets' on a microblogging service. Explain what a microblog is.

n) Explain what an email client is.

o) Sometimes Charlotte uses webmail instead of her email client. Explain why webmail can have advantages over an email client.

Exam-style Questions

8 Data is often input into a computer system by automatic methods such as OCR, OMR, smart cards, RFID and bar codes.

a) Explain why automated data input is often preferred to manual data entry at a keyboard.

b) Describe what OCR data input is.

c) Explain how OCR technology can be useful in traffic enforcement cameras.

d) Describe how OMR input differs from OCR.

e) State **two** situations where OMR is useful.

f) What is a smart card?

g) Explain why smart cards have replaced magnetic strips in many applications.

h) State **three** situations where smart cards are used.

i) Explain how RFID differs from a smart card.

j) Explain how RFID can be useful to a supermarket.

k) What is a bar code?

l) Explain how a bar code is used to help produce a supermarket itemised receipt.

m) Explain how the use of bar codes can help in investigating the shopping habits of individuals.

n) Explain the advantages and disadvantages of a supermarket having knowledge of your shopping habits.

Exam-style Questions

9 Look at the image below.

a) What type of data input is shown here?

b) Describe how the data in this example is input into a computer system.

c) State **two** other situations where data is input into a computer system in the same way.

10 State **two** reasons why most operating systems add extensions to file names.

11 A robot can be programmed to drive across the floor with some simple commands.
For example: Repeat 4 [fd 50 rt 90] draws a square. □

Draw the shapes traced by the following commands.

Commands	Result
a) repeat 5[fd 50 lt 360/5]	
b) repeat 7[fd 50 lt 360/7]	
c) repeat 8[fd 50 bk 50 rt 360/8]	
d) repeat 8[fd 50 bk 100 rt 45]	
e) repeat 4[fd 100 rt 90 bk 100]	
f) repeat 20[fd 50 bk 50 rt 360/20]	

Exam-style Questions

12 **a)** Bling is a small company that manufactures and sells jewellery. It takes orders online and keeps details of its stock, its suppliers and customers. It uses specially written database software for this purpose and also an office suite of programs for general purpose administration.

Bling employs an office manager, two office assistants and occasionally recruits temporary staff to help in the office at busy times. They use a general purpose office suite which consists of a word processor, a spreadsheet and presentation software. The managers of Bling are investigating the possibility of using specialist accounting software to handle cash flow and tax matters.

i) Describe how the office staff could benefit from using macros when producing documents for the company.

ii) Some letters have been sent out containing spelling mistakes, despite being spell checked by the software. Explain how this can happen.

iii) Explain **two** ways in which Bling might make use of presentation software to promote its goods.

b) Bling needs to update its database software. The management is considering whether to commission new software from a software developer, get Open Source software that has been written to handle general stock-taking functions, or make use of Software as a Service.

i) Describe how Software as a Service might be a good option for Bling.

ii) Explain why using Software as a Service may cause problems for Bling.

iii) What is Open Source software and why might Bling benefit from choosing to use it?

iv) Explain why using Open Source software for accounting purposes might be a dangerous option for Bling.

c) The managers of Bling often work with freelance designers to develop new products. They use Cloud computing to cooperate.

i) Explain what is meant by Cloud computing and why it is a good option in this case.

ii) Explain why the freelance designers need a broadband connection when discussing ideas with each other.

d) At the moment, Bling uses a spreadsheet to manage its finances and prepare invoices for customers. It has developed the design of this spreadsheet in-house over many years.

Explain why a spreadsheet developed in-house may pose problems for Bling.

Notes

facebook - advantages
|
easy
|
quick

Notes

Notes

Notes